FULL OF CARP

Hungry Mind Press
Saint Paul, Minnesota

Text © 1997 by Peter Bradley
Illustrations © 1997 by Hungry Mind Press

Carp illustration courtesy of the U.S. Fish and Wildlife Service

Published by Hungry Mind Press
1648 Grand Avenue
Saint Paul, Minnesota 55105

9 8 7 6 5 4 3 2 1
First Hungry Mind Press printing 1997

Library of Congress Catalog Number: 97-73780
ISBN: 1-886913-19-6

Printed in the United States of America

Cover design: Don Leeper
Book design: Will Powers
Typesetting: Stanton Publication Services, Inc.

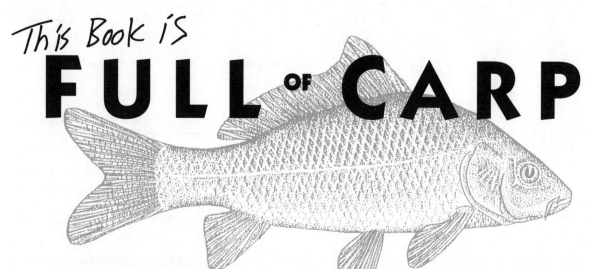

This Book is
FULL OF CARP

by Peter Bradley illustrated by Jeff Tolbert

For Barbara

It will quickly become apparent to the thoughtful reader that a work of this heroic scope necessitates conjuring well beyond the powers of a single individual. Hence, with gratitude and delight, I acknowledge the contributions of the following: my daughters, Laura and Carrie, whose spontaneous laughter at the start sustained me on an odyssey others might have viewed as a fool's errand; Jeff Hohman, whose immediate certainty and support buttressed my initially shaky conviction; friends and colleagues close by who caught carp fever and thereby enriched the content of this book; and finally, friends at a distance who have urged me over the years to engage more fully a seeming facility for writing. I realize that this may not be quite what they had in mind, but it's something.

FULL OF CARP

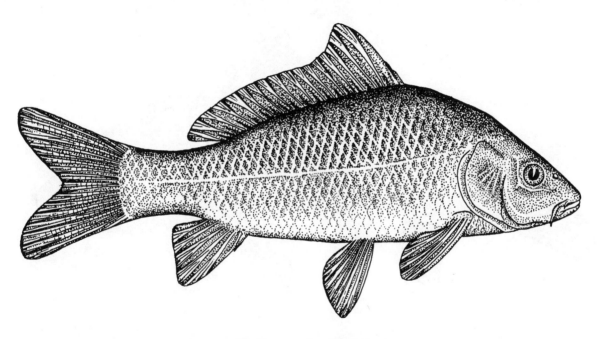

Your standard carp

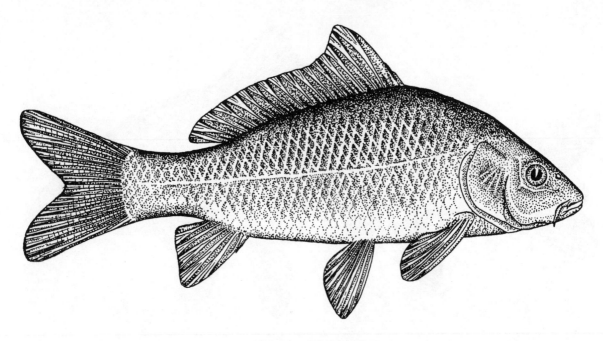

Same old carp

More of the same old carp

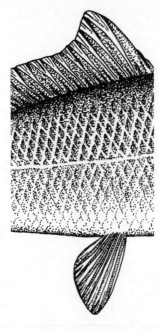

Piece of carp

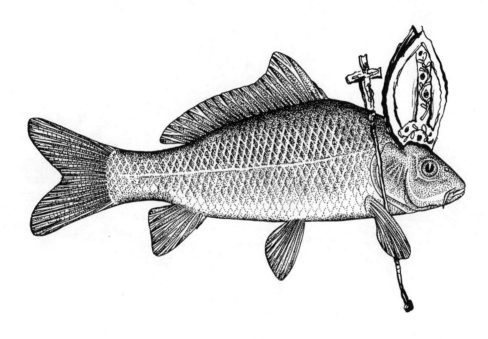

Holy carp

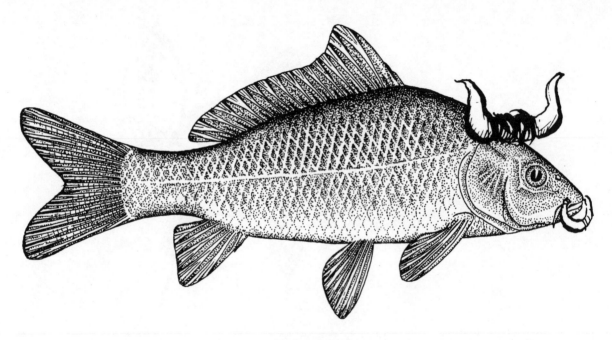

Bull carp

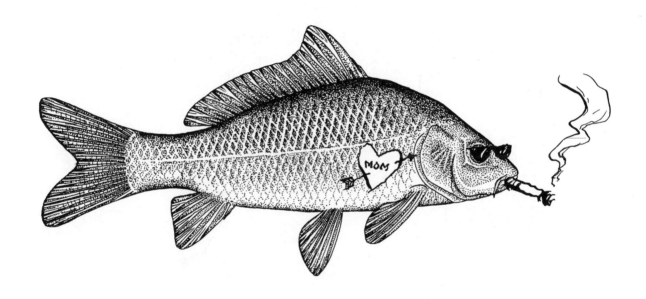

Tough carp

Giving a carp

Taking a carp

Not taking any more carp

Cut the carp

Carp happens

When the carp hits the fan

CARP FACT

The common carp, *Cyprinus carpio,* is a member of the minnow
family, as are goldfish. But carp frequently grow to a length of
forty inches and a weight of seventy pounds in Europe and Asia.
In England and the United States, the maximum weight
is about forty-five pounds. That is still a lot of carp.

Carpe diem *(Seize the day)*

Raining carps and dogs

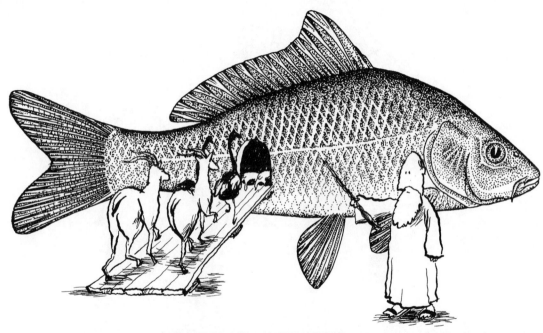

The boarding of Noah's Carp

The signing of the Magna Carpa

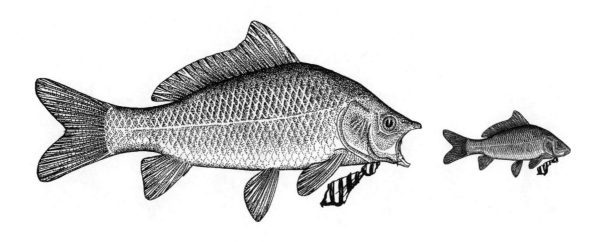

Carporate merger

Putting the carp before the horse

His carp is worse than his bite

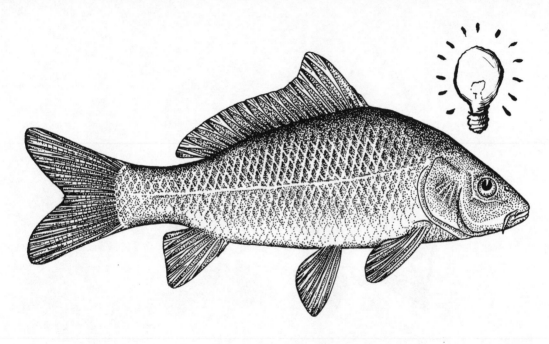

A carpy idea

Amusement carp

Magic carpet

Carp shoot

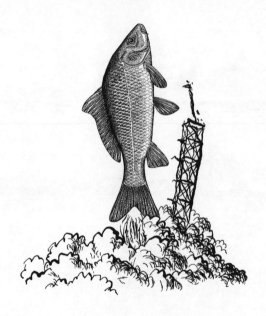

Carp Canaveral

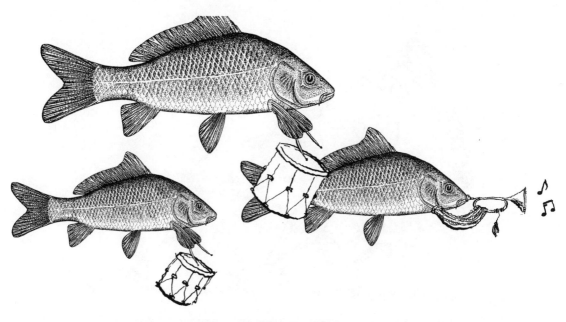

Drum and Bugle Carps

United States Marine Carps

Carpe blanche

CARP FACT

One of the earliest published recipes for carp appeared more than three hundred years ago in Izaak Walton's *The Compleat Angler*. Today, carp is a very popular food in Asia and Europe. It is largely eschewed in the United States. The explanation would seem to be a matter of taste.

Cornucarpia

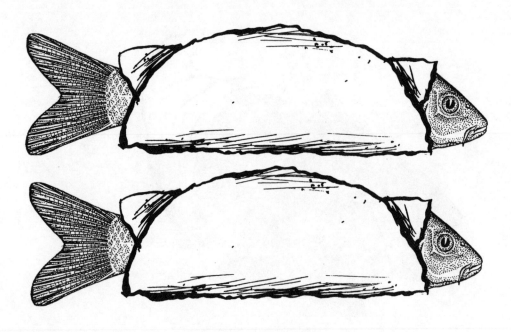

Carpes Suzette

Carpohydrate loading

Carpuccino

Carponated beverages

Pasta Carponara

Dining à la carpe

The carp's pajamas

Nightcarp

Stocking carps

Shopping carp

Carptop carrier

Carp pool

Tarot carp

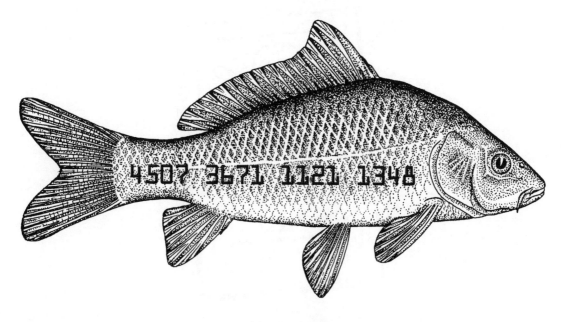

MasterCarp

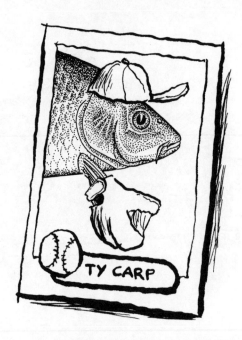

Baseball carp

Carpal tunnel syndrome

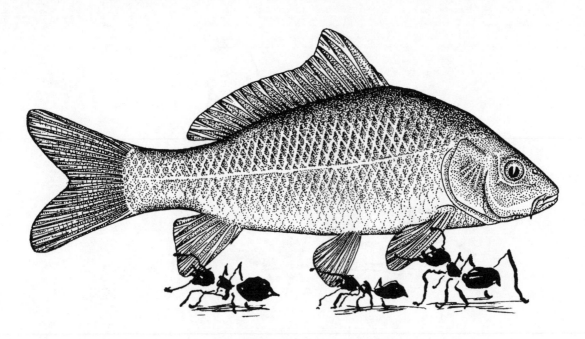

Carpenter ants

Pushcarp vendor

CARP FACT

Some ornamental carp,
such as champion Koi,
have been valued at
well over $50,000.
This is not chicken feed.

Al Carpone

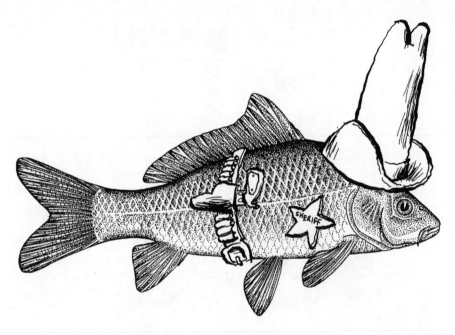

Wyatt Carp

Carpalong Cassidy

Joan of Carp

Napoleon Bonacarpe

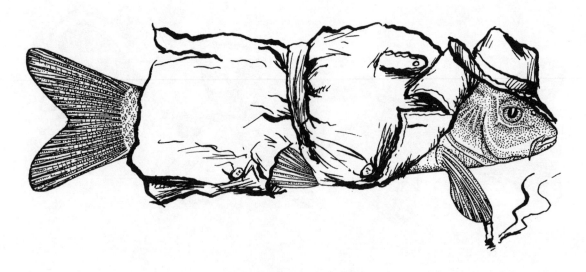

Humphrey Bocarp

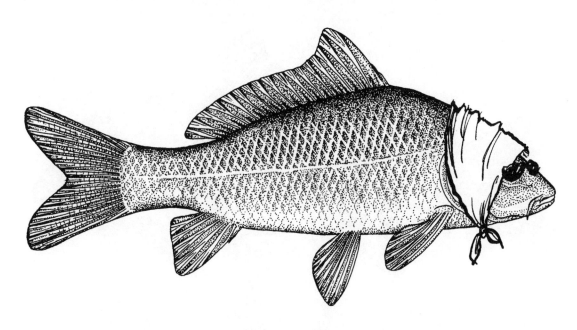

Greta Carpo

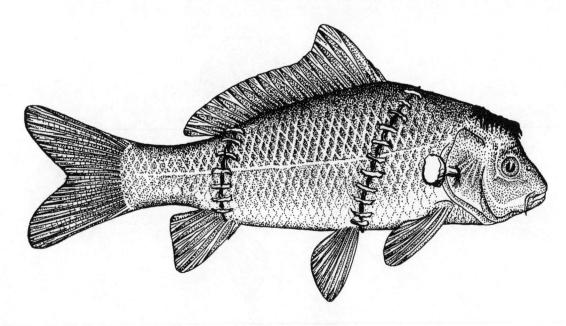

Boris Carploff

Franz Carpfka

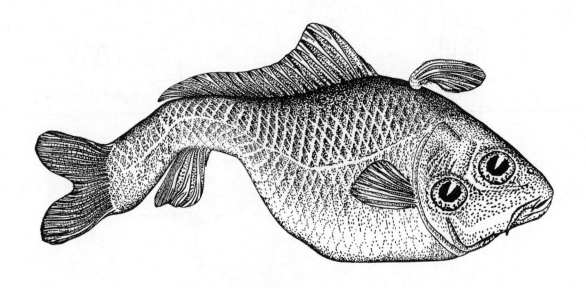

Pablo Picarpo

Carp artist

The Museum of Carp

BILLIONS
AND BILLIONS
OF STARS...

Carpl Sagan

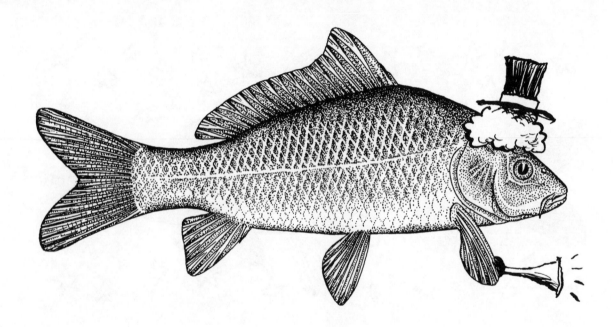

Carpo Marx

COGITO CARPUM
ERGO SUM

René Descarpes

Bert Carps

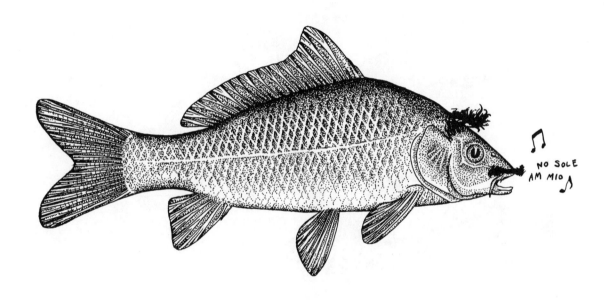

Enrico Carpuso

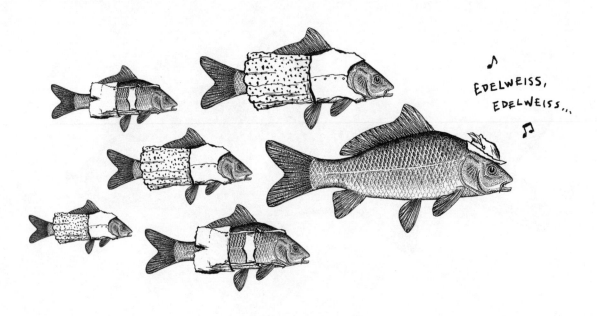

The Von Carpp family singers

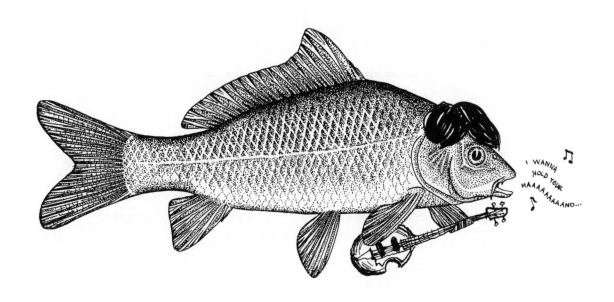

Paul McCarpney

CARP FACT

Carp were introduced in England in 1496
exclusively for the sporting pleasure of royalty.
Angry commoners felt this was an unjust imposition
of restricted carping.

Good carp, bad carp

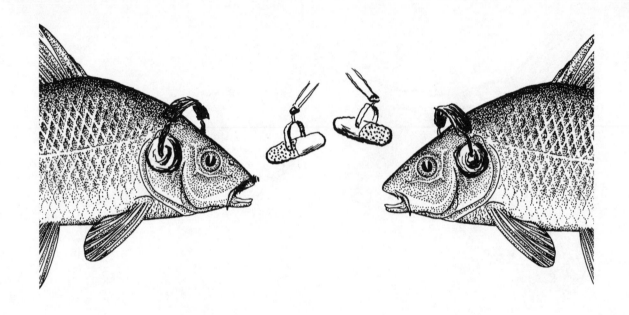

Carp Talk guys

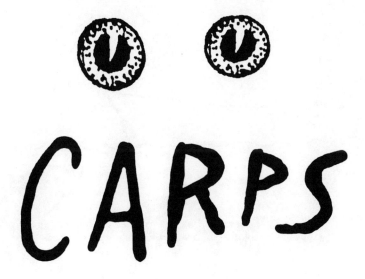

The Musical

The Carps of Wrath

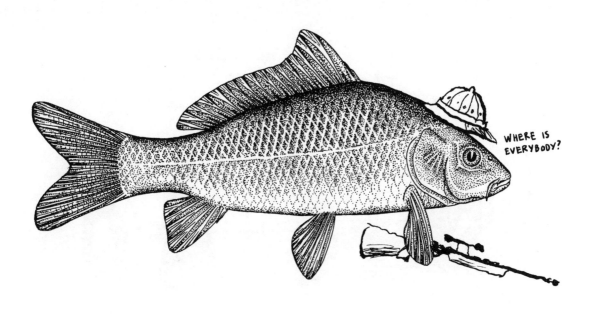

The Carp is a Lonely Hunter

Carp Fear

Jurassic Carp

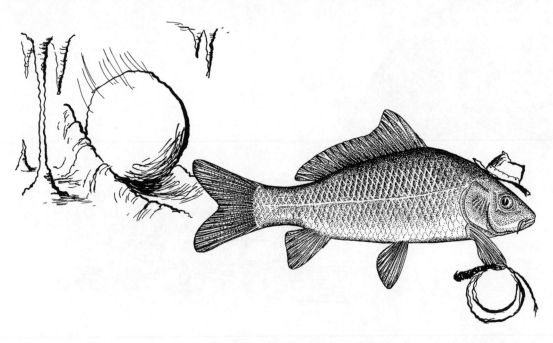

Raiders of the Lost Carp

The Carped Crusaders

MAKE IT SO...

Jean-Luc Picarp

Carp of Zorro

Carp on a Hot Tin Roof

A Streetcarp Named Desire

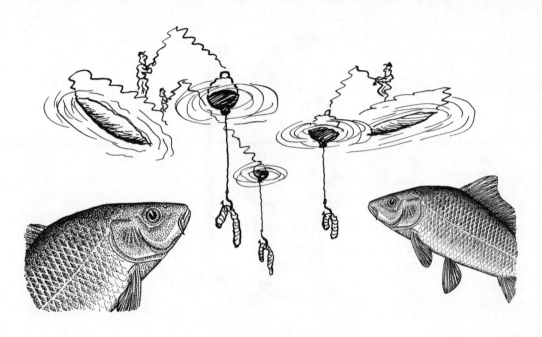

The World According to Carp

Fin